WALKING ON WATER

BY

PAMELA R. BRADLEY

Walking On Water
Pamela R. Bradley

DH Publishing Company
PO Box 333
Indianapolis, IN 46250

ISBN: 13: 978-1-7336502-3-6
ISBN: 10: 1-7336502-3-7

Cover Design by: DH Publishing Company
Editor: DH Publishing Company
www.dhpublishingco.com
Author: chefpambradley@yahoo.com

DH Books

Walking On Water
Pamela R. Bradley

Table of Contents

Walking On Water
Pamela R. Bradley

Walking On Water
Pamela R. Bradley

JESUS WALKS ON THE WATER

[2] Immediately Jesus made the disciples get into the boat and go on ahead of him to the other side, while he dismissed the crowd. [23] After he had dismissed them, he went up on a mountainside by himself to pray. Later that night, he was there alone, [24] and the boat was already a considerable distance from land, buffeted by the waves because the wind was against it. [25] Shortly before dawn, Jesus went out to them, walking on the lake. [26] When the disciples saw him walking on the lake, they were terrified. "It's a ghost," they said, and cried out in fear. [27] But Jesus immediately said to them: "Take courage! It is I. Don't be afraid." [28] "Lord, if it's you," Peter replied, "tell me to come to you on the water." [29] "Come," he said. Then Peter got down out of the boat, walked on the water and came toward Jesus. [30] But when he saw the wind, he was afraid and, beginning to sink, cried out, "Lord, save me!" [31] Immediately Jesus reached out his hand and caught him. "You of little faith," he said, "why did you doubt?" [32] And when they climbed into the boat, the wind died down. [33] Then those who were in the boat worshiped him, saying, "Truly you are the Son of God."

Walking On Water
Pamela R. Bradley

MY DAILY PRAYER

Dear Heavenly Father, I come to you as humble as I know how thanking you and praising you for being God all by yourself, and being the Alpha and Omega the beginning and the end. You knew me before you formed me in my mother's womb. I thank you for keeping me. You said you would never leave me nor forsake me. I say thank you for healing my body, oh God you said by your stripes I am healed. Thank you for providing a way for me, you said that you shall supply all my needs according to your riches and glory. Thank you for protecting me from danger seen and unseen. Thank you, God, for putting a hedge of protection around me. No weapon formed against me shall prosper and any evil word that comes up against me shall be condemned.

God, I love you for the unconditional love you have shown towards me when you shed your blood on Calvary. You did not have to do it, but you did. I thank you for your mercy and for your grace that's new every day. God, now please bless my kids, my granddaughter, my parents, and my family. God, thank you for my parents. Thank you for keeping them, and touching and healing their bodies from cancer. Thank you for restoring their bodies to good health and thank you for keeping them around so I can see the mighty hand you have done with them, and if you did it for them, you could do it for me. I say thank you, God, that you have protected my children and granddaughter. You said you would bless me and my children and my children's children, so I say thank you. Thank you for protecting my siblings from what could have been bad, but by your mercy and grace, you kept them, so I say Thank you. Thank you for your unmerited favor, oh God, that you have shown me. Thank you for the many doors you have opened, doors that no man can close because it was only you that opened them. And for that, I'm Grateful, oh God in Jesus name I pray, Amen.

Walking On Water
Pamela R. Bradley

FORWARD

Pam is one of the most courageous, inspirational, God-fearing women I have had the pleasure of crossing paths with. From high school until the present, I have watched Pam deal with life's adversities and yet remain confident and faithful to God. I'm reminded of a phrase she uses consistently, "I give God all the glory." Although her journey has been one of many challenges, Pam remains continuously un-defeated, against all the odds throughout her journey. As a former chef, serving has been her passion until her health failed. However, through my observation and relationship with Pam, I have often called her the "Proverbs 31 Woman," a woman of strength. Therefore, I would recommend this book written from the heart of a victorious, determined, God-fearing woman as a tool to help discover your life purpose. I believe that everyone that reads this book will be affected for life and equipped with the tools needed to become who they were uniquely created to be on purpose for their divine purpose.

Pastor Patricia A. Germany
Senior Associate Pastor, BS, MSM, LCC

Walking On Water
Pamela R. Bradley

AUTHOR BIO

My name is Pamela R. Bradley. I am currently 55 years of age, and I have two children, a son, daughter, and one granddaughter. I was born and raised in Indianapolis, Indiana. My parents also reside in Indianapolis, along with my two brothers and one sister. I am a graduate of Arlington High School and Michael's Beauty College. I also graduated from Indianapolis Chefs Academy.

After graduating from Beauty College, I worked in my mom's Beauty shop working there for over ten years, but I still needed more. I had several jobs such as H.H. Greg and FedEx. I always moved from position to position only to better myself, it may have seemed like I wasn't stable or couldn't keep a job, but that wasn't it, I just did that because I always tried to find more money to better my lifestyle and provide for my children.

After a little more soul searching, I wanted to go back to school to become a Chef, and I did just that. I graduated and worked at a very nice catering company. I also did some catering of my own.

Walking On Water
Pamela R. Bradley

TAKING THINGS FOR GRANTED

We take so many things for granted getting up every day in good health. I clearly remember when my life was great, I loved what I did, and I was feeling good about what I was doing and happy with myself. I was working hard to reach a goal. I was enjoying my journey. And this journey started back in 2006 when I went to culinary school. I was in a bad place in my life, and I knew I had to pray because I had decisions to make. I was getting laid off my job, and I had to do something because I had kids to take care of and I had bills. I had to have faith to take that first step. I was in a bad marriage and needed to make a lifetime decision that would affect me for the rest of my life. I knew my future depended on it. So God woke me up early one morning. I turned on the TV and there it was, there was an infomercial on, it was the Chefs Academy. I prayed and asked God to please show me what he wanted me to do, and when I saw that commercial my heart lit up and I said wow, that's it, I will be a Chef. I was excited, so I call the next day and set up an appointment. I went to tour the school, and I fell in love, literally because I saw myself there, going to school, and that's what happened I enrolled and finish with a 3.2 and a degree

Walking On Water
Pamela R. Bradley

MY STORY

After enjoying life and doing the very thing that made me happy, which was cooking. I realized I still was not making the money I wanted to in my career, so I searched and prayed for God to direct me in the direction I should go.

My marriage was failing for the second time, and I was unhappy and unsettling. I prayed without ceasing; that is what the Bible tells us to do. One day my answer came. I woke up one morning and went to the library and searched for a better job. I was led to the website Career Builder, and there it popped up right in my face. Norwegian Cruise line hiring, I said yeah right, I couldn't get a job like that it was out of town in Hawaii to be exact. I looked at the website, and the more I looked, the more excited I got, so what did I do, I applied and guess what, weeks later I receive an email saying they were interested in me and wanted to interview me. The catch was they had only certain states they were interviewing in, so I had to travel to Chicago, Illinois, for my interview. I was a little turned off because I had to make that sacrifice, but something told me to do it. I told my husband at the time and family, but I believe in the back of their mind they were saying yeah right, you are driving to Chicago to get an interview for a job on a Cruise-ship. I asked myself, who will ride with me, so at the time, I mentioned it to one of my girlfriends and she volunteered to go with me. Well, guess what, I went, and I was interviewed, and they hired me on the spot. They gave me a huge folder to complete. Completing the paperwork was a part of the hiring process and when I tell you the thought of having to do all that they were asking was a turnoff, but it will show how determined and how bad you wanted the job. I spoke to one of my male cousins, and he encouraged me to move forward with the process, so I did. I proceeded with everything, and it was all a success. Discipline and determination are what it takes to get me to that next step in the hiring process. I made it. I got the job. So now I just had to wait for the call for the next opening for training. I was working at Indiana Live Casino, and I continued working there until I got my call to leave, which came in Feb 2009. It was my time to go and to start my new journey in my Career. I was so excited at this time in my life and was ready to take on this major move because I needed it in my life. God had blessed me with that dream job any Chef would want to work on a Cruise ship.

My family gave me a going away party. One of my cousins volunteered and did that for me, I was very happy. That's when it became real, only tears flowing with family and friends, giving me their blessings and well wishes. My time had come to leave, and it was tough to let go of my daughter and granddaughter. My son, who was always the strong one, was fine. Even my husband was fine with me leaving so I thought.

Leaving early that morning traveling all by myself on such a long flight, I was not scared because I knew I was making the right decision because God had given me peace about it, so I was okay.

Walking On Water
Pamela R. Bradley

Walking On Water
Pamela R. Bradley

THE ARRIVAL AND TRAINING IN HAWAII

When I arrived at the ship, I was like wow! Oh, my God! It was so big I had never been so close to such a big boat in my life. This was my first cruise, and I ended up working on it, that's God. I talked to God, I asked, is this what you had in store for me? I would have never known it if I had not dared to jump outside the box. It was simply amazing, and my first job on the ship was in the buffet area that overlooked the ocean. My office every day was looking out and seeing all the beautiful water and beautiful sunsets, merely Amazing.

My career on the Norwegian cruise line, lasted around two years. My rotation was five months on and six weeks off. I enjoyed every moment of it, and it was my new career on the water. During that experience, it taught me accountability, discipline, and my faith grew stronger in the Lord. I stepped out on faith, and I had to surrender myself to God because when I faced challenges, I knew I had to depend on him. Working away from family and friends felt very lonely, and it was transparent. I was terrified and intimidated by such a big ship. I thought I would get lost with all the watertight doors, but God said he would never leave me nor forsake me, so I trusted him.
On the ship, we had to go to training for one week. It was very intense it entailed fire and safety with a written test, and at the end, we had to pass with at least 70%. I was never a smart student. I had to apply myself and study. My training took me back to school, and I had to focus and take notes. Things were going well my practical test was swimming and learning how to dive into the deep water, and how to get in and out of a raft. I was scared, but l did not let it show.

The weeks went by fast, we all studied, but you always knew who the brains of the class were, but I would not let them know I was trailing behind. I humbled myself and paired up with the strongest in the class. The time had come, the day of the test, yes, I was so nervous, and I did my best, but I failed

20

my test. The good news was I had one more time to retake it. I said Lord you didn't bring me this far to leave me, so I went further and got a tutor, someone that had passed the test. I had no shame because I knew that I had to pass this test, or I would be sent home. So I retook the test and passed it the second time. I was so happy and ready to start my new journey and career cooking on the water.

Walking On Water
Pamela R. Bradley

THE NEW CAREER COOKING ON THE WATER

My journey was amazing. I worked every day 10-12 hours a day, but I was still happy because I was living a dream in Hawaii. This was a dream come true, but in my life, I felt I always had to fight my way through something, through relationships, through finances, now through a health issue. I remember praying and asking God for patience because suddenly, I was going through everything. God would not bless me without a test. "Okay, you want patience, let's see if you can handle this situation," and there came another one. I got to where I said to God okay, I get it. I think I got this now, so there it was I had the patience of Job. I felt as if I could stay calm and ride the wave until that storm was over knowing this too shall pass.

Moving on in the season, I was in, I owed it to God. I was happier than I ever been in my entire life. God had chosen this path for me, and he was preparing me for greatness, and I didn't even know it. Years had passed, and my season was ending for my career on The Norwegian Cruise line. I left as a better person, stronger than ever because I accomplished what some people failed at, but God was on my side telling me I can do this. I'm a strong Christian woman with the favor of God! God said he would never leave me nor forsake me. I trusted God. Sometimes, I got weak, and I cried, yes, I cried in Hawaii the place of love and beauty all around. I did because I was going through a lot of problems I left at home that still followed me to Hawaii. I pressed and pressed my way through; I had to focus daily on my job. I continued to pray every day before I left my cabin because I never knew what my day would entail.

After I passed my test and I became a permanent full-time employee. It was seven days a week, 10 to 12 hours a day. What changes did I have to make? I ate right and exercise and accomplishing those two things made my life a better place to live. I felt good and powerful and let's not forget I felt very confident in myself no low self-esteem. As young girls growing up we take on spirits, we shouldn't have to deal with, like bullying, not fitting in with most girl clicks as they called it. The spirit of jealousy for no reason, if they only knew the things I had to endure. See women judge a book by its cover instead of taking some time out to get to know a person. They see a pretty girl that

Walking On Water
Pamela R. Bradley

keeps herself up and her hair is pretty, but they didn't see a girl shy with low self-esteem and no confidence in herself. It took me to go through many relationships trying to find someone to fill that void I had in my spirit. Since I'm lead to writing everything in my spirit, I will throw this out there. My father asked me one day what happened to me. Why I couldn't keep a man? They have been married for 50 years and asked me what happened to me? But now I wonder why I went through two marriages and they both were failed marriages. Well now I see how important it is for daughters to have their fathers or a strong father figure in their life that will show her how a man should treat a woman. That builds character and confidence in her. Then she will learn her worth at an early age.

Through the years after making tons of mistakes, I got tired. I was raised in the church and my grandmother would take us to Sunday school Church and BTU after church service so we would be in church all day. I thank God for all of that; I didn't understand it then, the question I would ask myself, "Dang grandma does it take all of this. Why do we have to go to church so much?" Now I know, and now I understand why it took all of that, why, so we would be equipped for the challenges of the world today. Been introduced to God at an early age and baptized at 8 has made me the woman of God I am today.

I came home from the cruise ship, happy to be back with my family and granddaughter. I had big hopes of finding that good job in the kitchen as a Sous Chef or even just running my own business. I tried hard to look for that job, but meanwhile, I knew I could go back to the catering job I had when I was in school, and where I did my internship. I had a good reputation there, and I could always return if I needed to, so that's what I did, and I still searched for that ideal job for me. I got on the website to numerous sites for employment as I continued to work and was happy doing what I did. I did not realize I had a different attitude this time, I had gained a lot of confidence so I walked with my head up and feeling like I can conquer anything I set my mind to do. Time went on then, and I finally got a job at a cute Breakfast Café, which I just loved. I loved it because I saw myself running it. I can do something like this. I worked hard on that job and wanted what I deserved, I knew I was qualified now I had a Culinary degree, and I have experience on a Cruise ship cooking for thousands of people. I deserved a good paying job. Well, the pay barely paid my bills. I had to work every holiday, drove long miles to work in the winter time, and it was crazy driving through the snow,

Walking On Water
Pamela R. Bradley

but I did it. And I forgot to mention I had to work with all female cooks. Why did they feel intimidated? Women are so quick to judge a book by its cover because of their insecurities. Now God has blessed me with confidence in myself knowing I can do all things through Christ who strengthens me, so don't get intimidated by me, it's the God in me, I didn't do this. We cannot be intimidated by a woman's glory if you don't know her story.

After searching my blessing came, I went back on the water, I tried hard to stay on land, but it didn't happen. God still had another plan. My time came, and I had to leave. Everything was too simple they skyped me for an interview, and I got the job at the highest pay for the cook, but I did not realize that until I got on the job. It was on my name badge, then everybody started asking, is she a cook 1, and started acting jealous. A black woman strong and confident, in my head I was saying you all don't know I got this. The male cook was ready to push me around and tried to bully me but I gave them a fight every time and sometimes in a nice way, but it would depend on how many chances I gave you to let up on me. My experience working in the kitchen was awesome; it was rough, but it made me a stronger person. You know the old saying "if you can't stand the heat, get out of the kitchen," That's such a true statement, it's no place for the weak, you have to be strong, confident, and show that you can be a team player and know how to multi-task. I learned to stand up and be confident in everything I did. If you don't, you will be walked over, and people don't have a problem trying to make you look like a fool. I learned to only be around positive energy that's the only way to make it. I let my light shine, no matter what. So I was the light on my job, and God revealed that so I could handle the challenges that came my way. Was it easy, no it wasn't, it was a day by day process. But I wouldn't be who, or where I am today if it wasn't for every tear, every disappointment, and every heartbreak situation, yes all that, I wouldn't be where I am today. Okay, so let's stop right here and have church because when I look back over my life, and I think things over, I can say that I've been blessed, I got a testimony! I see so clearly now that everything that I have been through God orchestrated every bit of it, I can see it. I really can say I understand every word of that song because God put me through the TEST so I could have a testimony. Life was good and I was living my dream making money, and I am happy. I haven't felt like this in the past seven years. I could almost say this was the best years of my life. It was a long time coming for me to be happy learning to love myself feeling confident and strong, and strong in my mind, my body, and my soul. We need all of that to survive. Can't leave out anything because one doesn't work without the other. If you are weak in your mind, you are weak in your body, then that tears into your soul. We have to learn to love ourselves so we will always put ourselves first, this may sound selfish, but it's self love, and if you can't love yourself, who else will love you.

Walking On Water
Pamela R. Bradley

SHARING THE NEWS WITH MY FAMILY

I was diagnosed with Breast Cancer in November 2013, and my surgery was scheduled for February 3, 2014. I was at Macy's on Black Friday with my granddaughter when I received the phone call from my nurse just after having my annual mammogram. She explained to me that my biopsy came back positive. I was diagnosed with stage four Breast Cancer. I had to sit down with tears streaming down my face. But at some point, I had to pull myself together because of my granddaughter Nanna was with me. Seeing me cry, she cried. But all I could say was, "Baby, I am okay." I later pulled myself together and left the store. When I made it to my car, I discovered I was in tears again, and that went on for like a minute. Then, afterward, I made some phone calls to share the horrible news. I began to call my family and share the news. My mom was shocked and she tried to calm me down and tell me that I would be fine.

I was scheduled to return to work on that Sunday because I was working on the American Queen Riverboat; cooking and cruising the Mississippi River. Despite being reluctant in sharing the ordeal, I knew I would have to share it with my Executive Chef and my coworkers after returning to work. And the longer I tried keeping the news to myself, the worse I felt. However, after sharing the news to them, I thank God they were all supportive. Finally, I got a grip on what was going on, and I told myself, Pam, this could have been worse, having been diagnosed with breast cancer didn't sound too bad. But I had little information about the ailment, but I decided to be optimistic.

After scheduling to meet with my Oncologist, I summoned enough courage to go by myself. And on getting there, he asked if anyone was with me, and I answered by saying, "No." But I was surprised to hear him say, "Well, you will need a support system." I got nervous again. I explained to him I have one, then he enlightened me on the type of breast cancer I had thought wasn't so bad. He cautiously explained that he would need to remove the left breast, where the lump was located. While he continued talking, I also told him I wanted the right breast removed as well; and in my mind, I was thinking, I never want to go through this ordeal again. And, eventually, I was scheduled for a double mastectomy. I cried all the way home after leaving the doctor's office. I had to tell my two children; though my son was in Los Angeles and I couldn't even have the courage to talk to him, I had to text him, knowing that he would hurt more, hearing me relay the message to him. The news hit him, but he pulled it all together so as not to let that affect me more. I couldn't even get it out when I was about to tell my daughter, but my mom was with me, and she had to help out by telling her. On hearing the news, my daughter instantly broke down in tears, crying profusely. I knew I had to be strong for her, and thanks to God, I was. Trying to accept what I was diagnosed with made me cry every day, and I meant every day! My prayer then was, Lord, please bring me back after surgery; and this is because I had no major surgery where I would have to be out. Thinking about it, always sent a frightening feeling through me. All I could do then was to pray to God; I prayed and prayed for peace, and I get this on Monday morning, which was the day of my surgery, I was just happy smiling like nothing was about to happen. And that was when I knew God was with me and that he had answered my prayers. However, going back for a minute, this question did come to my mind, "Why me, Lord? What did I do to deserve this?" But that is not the God we serve. The book of *Psalms 34:19 says, "Many are the afflictions of the righteous: but the Lord delivereth him out of them all,* so ask yourself: Why not, you? God is bigger than cancer. God has allowed me to live through what many people died from, and that was Grace provided for me, even when I didn't deserve it. *Psalms 34:8 says, "oh, taste, and see that The Lord is great, blessed is the man that trusteth in him."* Everyone from the doctors to the nurses was all a blessing. I knew they were all God sent.

The Scripture says in Deuteronomy 31:8 NIV: The Lord himself goes before you and will be with you; he will never leave you nor forsake you. Do not be afraid; do not be discouraged. I'm only here because of God's Mercy and Grace, not because of anything I did, *Hebrews 11:1 "Faith is the substance of things hoped for the evidence of things unseen."* Faith without works is dead. I knew I had to have the faith the size of a mustard seed like the word says. It's all I needed, so I stood by that. Proverbs 3:5-6 And I knew I had to trust in the Lord with all my heart and lean not on my own understanding but acknowledge him and all my ways and he shall direct my path.

Walking On Water
Pamela R. Bradley

AFTER THE SURGERY

After my surgery, which was a success, I woke up praising God because it was over. After staying in the hospital for only one day, I went home to recover, and each day I felt better, and, giving thanks to God, scaling me through the hurdles of the operation. However, as time goes on with me, being around every day, reality set in, the devil wanted me to stress over my bills since I wasn't working. But my God said '*He would supply all my needs according to his riches and Glory Philippians' 4:19* and that was exactly what he did. I had enough money to do everything I needed to do. *Matthew 6:9-13; Our Father which is in heaven, hallowed be thy name thou kingdom come;* this scripture was the scripture I prayed daily for peace. *Psalm 23 The Lord is my shepherd, I shall not want*; I knew I had to speak this scripture in my spirit, so that I would lack for nothing. Going through this journey in my life had taught me more about leaning and trusting God totally, especially knowing that no one else could get me through the situation as God could. Another favorite scripture I had to get in my spirit was: *Now to him who is able to do exceedingly abundantly above all that we ask or think, according to the power that works- Ephesians 3:20-21.*

Strong faith is what we need to get through whatever situation we may be going through. I know it's easier said than done, but we must still exhibit faith to scale successfully through life's challenges. Usually people say they have faith without putting it to work. But, remember that the word says, "Faith without works is dead." James 2:14: What does it profit, my brethren, men says he has faith but does not have works? I didn't know this, but February 3, 2014, was my moment to shine according to God's word in Matthew 5:16; Let your light shine before men, that they may see your good works, and glorify your Father which is in heaven. And also according to *Psalms 27:1, "The Lord is my light and my salvation; whom shall I fear? The Lord is the strength of my life; of whom shall I be afraid?"* We serve a sovereign God, and he is far bigger than every situation put together. I recovered, and living, and enjoying my life as expected.

Walking On Water
Pamela R. Bradley

LIFE HAPPENED AGAIN

As a cancer survivor, I had returned to work, feeling good, and not looking like anything happened for quite a period. But suddenly, life happened again. I was diagnosed again, this time of stage 4 Breast Cancer, and it had spread all over my body. This time, it had gotten into my bones and fractured my vertebrae.

It all began after I had my last surgery done, which was the nipple transplant. I had that done in February 2016 because I had reconstructed surgery and it looks like everything was fine, even though I had felt something weird in my breast before the surgery. But I went ahead with the surgery, and I proceeded since my doctor said nothing was wrong. The surgery went fine, but two weeks after, everything began. I woke up one morning with a pain in my back that didn't go away, I was at home on vacation and I did everything I could think of for the pain to go away. I later returned to work with that pain in my back and still got up every day for work until I couldn't take it anymore. They finally did a CT scan on me, and they said cancer had reached my bones. I was told I had fractured vertebrae, and I was done, and all I could utter was, "No Way!"

To cut the long story short, I had to leave my job on the Riverboat. I went home to see my doctor again, and he ordered a CT and PET scan. Then he explained what it was and told me I had to have a back surgery first; and if not, it would leave me paralyzed. After then, I had pain in my neck, meaning cancer already moved to my spine. And that meant a neck surgery was inevitable. I eventually had the operations, and I wore a neck brace for six weeks. I recovered from both the surgeries, but after removing the neck brace, I discovered that I had lost a little range of sensitivity and flexibility in my neck, and I couldn't move my neck like I ought to, and that made me shed more tears. I didn't want to accept my new status as normal.

Honestly, I hated it every morning, waking up with my head feeling so heavy to the point I thought I could fall over. But God was sufficient for me by helping me get a grip on the situation. I'm so blessed to be alive and not paralyzed. "I will bless the Lord at all times, and his praises shall continually be in my mouth." Psalms 34:1.' Though I had no time to think about what I was about to face before my surgeries; and afterward, I couldn't walk by myself nor clean myself up, I was a mess. And an emotional mess, but with all the pain Meds I was on, I just slept throughout the day.

After my surgery, I went straight into radiation, and 25 treatments of radiation. I wasn't thinking about side effects, and no one warned me about them either. All they said was, stay strong. Well, because of the result of radiation, I became so sick, my stomach couldn't keep nothing down, and it got to where I was scared even to eat. I became so weak, and I lost so much weight, one day, my physical therapist came over to check on me. She called my doctor, and I ended up in the ER; however, I didn't know my condition was that bad. I stayed for over a week as my situation was worse than I ever imagined, and this is because I had esophagus problems, which prevented me from passing food down due to the radiation.

After taking tons of medication and after completing radiation, I finally felt much better. I was walking better, and I did something on my own. I was feeling more like myself. God allowed me to live through this, and I have to keep stressing that. Yes, I made it! After one year, which included the five weeks of radiation and chemo every three weeks, three surgeries, two procedures, and a lot of pain MEDs, I'm still standing on God's word he will restore me back to good health.

I finally completed the chemo, and it was by the grace of God because my doctor kept telling me he wanted me to stay on that chemo called Taxotere for the rest of my life, or as long as my body can take it. But I am no longer on Taxotere because my body couldn't take it anymore, and also, I ended up with neuropathy in both hands, but it was worse in my left hand. I also ended up with fluid in my lungs, which caused me to have shortness of breath and coughing. But I thank God I'm still here.

I was getting anxious and was feeling like I wanted a second opinion to be sure everything was okay. I prayed about it and felt good about it. So, I did just that to make sure I was okay, I contacted the Cancer treatment of America. I didn't have the mentality of them telling me any other news. However, they did find something, but I have to say, I'm so blessed because if I hadn't taken that step, the issue would have gone too long unnoticed, and that might have made me not to be here today. They found a small spot on my brain from the MRI. It was small, and I only needed one treatment of radiation. And discovering on time made me say, "Thank you, Jesus, for the insight given to me to give the second opinion a trial."

Walking On Water
Pamela R. Bradley

After returning home, I had my appointment with my oncologist, and he then explained the reason they didn't schedule that MRI test. He said it was because I had no symptoms. I want to lay emphasize on this point because the thought of waiting until I had symptoms would have probably been too late. So I screamed at the top of my lungs, "Thank you, Jesus! Thank you, Jesus!" I have learned so much about this Cancer I have tagged it "the demon itself," because it aims to kill if you and don't catch it in time. When you have any symptoms, it may be for several reasons, and it could be the Cancer is growing and spreading.

Cancer, no doubt, is very painful and even more painful when it has progressed without you noticing the symptoms. Thinking back two years ago, and doing some comparative analysis with the present situation, I had it the first time with a Mammogram, but with no symptoms because it was at stage zero, and it was stabilized. This time, I can remember that, it felt like shooting pains going through my left breast, and it did scare me, and that led me to call my doctor. That, right there was my symptoms, so the deadly evil disease was probably getting bigger and busted out, then spread all over my body. I could remember that it was in my back, neck, shoulders, skull, brain, liver, and lungs, among other sections of my body. It was merely aiming to kill me, but Thanks to God, I am still standing today and as a two-time Breast Cancer Survivor.

Walking On Water
Pamela R. Bradley

THANK YOU JESUS!

I need you to hear this again. Yes! Jesus, you have been so good! Your mercy, made the situation not to consume me, and you saved me from what most people die from, and I thank you. I'm so filled with joy right now. I can't tell it all. Despite being diagnosed with Stage 4 Breast Cancer, the second battle with this disease, and I'm still here. Look at me; this did not destroy me. I hope I can help somebody because some people think God is not relevant to their situation. If you must know, it's God saving my life, and, restoring me back to good health according to his word. I will walk in victory every day, and I will live to the fullest of God's glory. Because of hurt and pain experienced from previous relationships I have been healed and has caused me to draw myself into some situations I never imagined. I now realize I should have given myself enough time to heal between relationships before jumping into another..

However, I sometimes wish I could turn back the hand of time, and even when I think about it, I always concluded that sometimes, such things are ordained to be; and aside from the 'not so good aspect,' such situation boosts one's courage to run, fight, and live life as expected.

Walking On Water
Pamela R. Bradley

SCRIPTURES THAT GOT ME THROUGH

II Thessalonians 2-15: Vs.15 "So then, brothers and sisters, stand firm and hold fast to the teachings we passed on to you, whether by word of mouth or by letter."

Jeremiah 30:17: "For I will restore health unto thee, and I will heal thee of thy wounds, saith the LORD; because they called thee an Outcast, saying, This is Zion, whom no man seeketh after."

Psalms 55:22 "Cast your cares on the Lord, and he will sustain you; he will never let the righteous be shaken."

Psalms 41:3; "The Lord sustained them on their sickbed and restores them from their bed of illness."

Jeremiah 29:11, "For I know the plans I have for you; declares the Lord!"

Philippians 4:13 "I can do all things through Christ which strengthens me."

Philippians 4:19: "But my God shall supply all your need according to his riches in glory by Christ Jesus."

Matthew 17:20 He replied, "Because you have so little faith. Truly I tell you, if you have faith as small as a mustard seed, you can say to this mountain, move from here to there,' and it will move; and nothing will be impossible for you."

Psalms 118:17: "I shall not die, but live, and declare the works of the Lord."

Walking On Water
Pamela R. Bradley

FAITH: THE ONLY TOOL

I wake up every day feeling like every day is a celebration. I wake up because God didn't have to let me live. I do not look like what I have been through, and I thank God. People often say that, and before this situation, I said that, too. But now it's a whole new level. I had fractured my vertebrae and neck. I had to wear a neck brace and walked with a walker and a belt around my waist, just in case I fell, they could pick me up.

The testimony I realized throughout my journey in sickness is I had to press on. I kept my faith. I cried all the time, but I knew I had to keep my faith. I heard one person say, "What do I do? I'm numb because I have been battling with my faith." When I heard that, I realized then how blessed I was. I knew the only thing I had going for me was my faith. I had people praying for me, so if I would not have faith that God could do it, then what's the point of praying? Faith is the substance of things hoped for and the evidence of things not seen. Faith will carry you through.
I can't go back to yesterday because I'm not that same girl. I can't go back as I came into the wonderland because I'm not that girl anymore. I wandered into my promise; thank God for the promise of "do not touch my anointed," I was built for this!

Don't be distracted by your suffering and keep your heart with God. Don't move it away from God. Offenses will come as a stumbling block or a stepping stone. Be diligent and dedicated.
Keep your heart with diligence. Beloved, think it not strange about the fiery trial to try you, as though some strange thing happened unto you. 1st Peter 4:12

Act 14:22: "Confirming the souls of the disciples, and exhorting them to continue in the faith, and that we must through much tribulation enter into the kingdom of God.
We must enter the kingdom of God through Tribulations. The word is medicinal; the more you read it, the more you get healed.

Walking On Water
Pamela R. Bradley

Suffer for the name of Jesus (Acts 5 41-42 paraphrased).

My situation is not for me alone; it is to encourage somebody else. I am a soldier. Job 1:20 Job fell and worshipped. He had a right to be distracted, but he wasn't.

God use me: I don't know what you would have me to do, but heal me and prosper me. I want to make a difference in someone's life. You kept me here for a reason: to spread Your goodness and I can't and won't sit on it. Give me the words to say, and I will continue to write down my words, and one day, I will have enough for a book.

Walking On Water
Pamela R. Bradley

LIFE AFTER CANCER

Life after Cancer, life after your Journey or whatever sounds best to you. Either way, you say it, it is the biggest challenge you have to face. I will speak for myself. It was the biggest challenge I had to face. I was insecure, and just a little bit scared. Yes, I said that my spirit was afraid because I could not move my neck. I got up every day, and I promise you it felt like I was carrying something big on my head. I cried, and I said God, how am I supposed to live like this? What do you want me to do feeling like this? My whole life was turned upside down. I said God you could have done anything else, but why did you take my range of motion? I can't turn around and look behind me, why God? Then I was trying to think of people with cancer and if they had any disability from the result of It. I could not think of anyone. After time had passed, I felt better, and I would push myself as hard as I could to get past that stage. All I could do was think about my kids, especially my granddaughter, who was with me from day 1. She was with me when I got the call. I said, God, please let me live. I don't want to die. I did things differently. I got up every day like I was going somewhere. One of my girlfriends said Pam, act like you're getting up to go to work and clean yourself up, put on your clothes and start there, so I did just that, and it became such a habit. I got up fixed my hair looked the best I could or whatever made me feel better is what I did, and it worked. I still do the same thing today. One day at a time each day got better for me. I would have to shower then sit down to rest and then put my clothes on, everything I did, I had to space it out so I would not wear myself out.

Walking On Water
Pamela R. Bradley

THREE TIMES CANCER AND SURVIVED

Irrespective that my life was going great, I was diagnosed with Breast Cancer on November 16, 2018 and that makes it the third time. Although I was still going to Philadelphia every three weeks for my treatments, I was looking and beginning to feel good. And I had traveled by myself. My doctors were even surprised at my quick mental and physical recovery, and they would compliment me.

I went for my regular six week medical checkup. I traveled for the checkup by myself, but my son would tell me to call him as soon as I collected the results of the tests. Aside from my son, I spoke to before the test, I also discussed it with a friend. Before I go further, I would like to say my son and my daughter has always been there for me. My parents were also there for me and both are cancer survivors. Their care for me has always amazed me, and I appreciate God for that privilege. Back to the test; I received the results and discovered that my ailment affected around three spots on my brain.

My doctor came out and said, "You made a turn for the worst." I was surprised, and the only thing I could say was, "What?" But what could I have done in such a situation other than to hear him out and hope for the best? So after explaining and showing me all the information connected to the test, they gave me their prognosis and sent me to radiation. And there I would be given a medical mask also with the radiation treatment; it would help to alleviate the condition. This mask was done in such a way to cover my face during radiation, and mind you, I was scared, but I had to face the fear because it's for my benefit. I had to overhaul my mind and think optimistically about the gadget used on me, I found my peace and I had to meditate on it, and that got me through. And that was when I understood that certain situations would always be there to make you learn as well as to help you put your trust in God. They eventually completed the treatment, and I was about to leave the health center to go back home when I suddenly broke down in tears, saying, "Oh my God, not again! Am I going to fight this thing all over again?" Afterwards, I went into one room to talk with one of the Navigators to talk to her and that even made me cry harder, but I had to pull myself together. And then it was time for me to leave the Cancer Center and fly back home with bad news. The flight back home was smooth, though I tried sleeping but couldn't.

When I arrived at my destination airport, my son picked me up. And like I said earlier, he has always been a caring, smart, and wise young man. When I got in the car, we talked, and he told me; "Momma, are you just bothered because the doctor said you made a turn for the worse? Well, compared to how you were doing, they didn't think you would make it this far." And he continued by saying, "Let me remind you that you made it up to 18 months after your surgery, you had fractured your vertebrae, your neck was broken, and you went through radiation treatment and Chemo. Those are evidence that you have come a long way; God has blessed you this far, and he will continually bless you." He said I should see this as another process. When I made it back home to talk to my parents, I didn't cry when I told them what the doctor said, and then I went upstairs to rest.

I woke up early the next morning when it dawned on me, I couldn't be upstairs alone, and I cried. I needed someone or somebody's arms around me, so I went downstairs to my parents' room and lay across the bed, and all I could do was cry. My daughter was over at the time and also heard me crying and asked me what was wrong. I explained the situation to her, and she also cried. Despite the fact I have been doing great without pain pills, I experienced a throbbing headache. I then realized I couldn't get too emotional because my head would hurt. And according to the doctor's result of cancer, my head might not further combine well with the emotional sobbing and crying. I also felt the urge not to go to church that morning because I would get emotional. So I stayed out a few Sundays, but then I later went, and I was fine. However, I was a little bit worried because those headaches were no joke. But I felt relaxed when I remembered the Bible verse that says: *"It is of the Lord's mercies that we are not consumed because his compassions fail not."* **Lamentations 3:22**

As I continued to move ahead in this journey, I realized there are a lot of distractions and constraints, that I wasn't aware of that made the journey so challenging. A frequent question that would always come to my mind then was how could things become so hard in life? But, it took God to sit me down so I can see what was going on in connection to the level of care I was getting from my family and friends. Fighting for my life has never been something I thought of doing, I have so much time on my hands to think about everything and everybody. If only I could change the world, we all would love each other

Walking On Water
Pamela R. Bradley

as God loves us with the Agape Love, which is an unconditional love. But that's too easy to do. There exist so much unforgiveness in the world, and that is sickening. I have learned that forgiveness is not really for others, but it's for you. The quicker you forgive a person, the faster you can move on in love with your life. Forgiving someone doesn't mean you continue bringing up the situation repeatedly with anger in your spirit, No! That's not it. You have to operate in love (The Agape Love); the only love that endures all things.

I have seen and witnessed it in my family and others; I'm not perfect, but I know I have a good and pure heart. I love everybody and like to see everyone love me, but that's not how the world works. There's always going to be someone that does not like you, and that is a fact about life. However, keeping God first in every situation gets us through anything. Since I have been home fighting my way through Breast Cancer, I learn in my family that although we love ourselves, we still lack the true Agape love.

I had just moved into my apartment in March 2016, right before I was diagnosed in May 2016, and the apartment was enough for me. I was trying hard to get my things together because I was ready to return home and to also find a job just on the mainland because my job had me traveling. I had been working on a Riverboat for almost four years. After I was diagnosed with cancer for the second time, I still held on to my apartment for that time, and even when I had to go for two surgeries, my apartment was still there. But after a while, it became challenging because it was a lot for my family to keep running back and forth to stay with me as they all were taking turns to take care of me, despite the inconveniences they might be experiencing, and that made me feel helpless. Still, I could not comprehend how my life had taken a turn for the worst. I was living my life and was happy with it. But I didn't realize there would be a time I would have to decide on whether I would keep my apartment or not. I had been staying with my parents to make it easy for everybody, and then the time came I had to decide to keep my apartment or give it up. All that was on my mind. I wanted my apartment because getting back to feeling normal again was so important. I cried and prayed about it, and there it was, God had answered my prayer. I gave up my apartment. I expressed my intention to my parents. I didn't want to give up my apartment. I was planning to hand over the supposed rent for my apartment to them, to help out in any way I can. All I wanted was to live a comfortable life anywhere, but not bring about any form

Walking On Water
Pamela R. Bradley

of confusion, friction, or inconveniences in the house, such as my parents' house. After reflecting for a while on whether to give up my apartment or not, I finally concluded and moved in with my parents.

My spirit was weak, and I didn't need the extra stress on where I would live. At this very moment, I felt like, where is my husband? My spirit was screaming, I wish I had a husband in my life to take care of me. Many nights I lay in my bed wishing I had my man's arms around me to comfort me, but I didn't get that. I had to lean totally on God to comfort me. Going through this journey was such a scary place, but once again, I had to trust in the Lord with my whole heart. All people would say was, "Girl, you are so strong." I wanted to say, "No, I'm not; I'm just fighting for my life the best way I know how." I knew my life depended on me staying positive and focused, no matter what. I often would lay in bed and rock myself to sleep just like a baby. I did not care whatever it took to comfort me; I just did.

People have made statements like they wondered why God did this to me. I felt like it was something I had done. So I confessed my sins to the Lord; fornication, adultery, and cussing (that was the worst of me); but then I thought to myself, if God punishes us for every sin we commit, then we would all be suffering from some type of disease because we all fall short of the glory of God. So, I had to tell myself, let no one try to tear you down because we all sin; nobody has lived a perfect life. Was I proud of what I did? No, I wasn't! But I see now that it's not worth it. I was doing my thing because it made me happy, and I never felt that love before ever in my life. But still it was wrong in God's sight, and I knew I was one of God's chosen ones. I just felt it in my spirit.

I was baptized at eight, and I was filled with the Holy Ghost. I loved church; my grandmother kept us in church, Sunday school morning services and then BTU afternoon service; I have been in church all my life. I knew better for doing wrong, but once again, I was living my life the best I knew, and I was not perfect. I have been married twice. The first marriage lasted nine years, and the second one lasted 13 years. If I could do it all over again, I honestly don't know what I would have done differently, because I felt I did everything possible to make it work. I loved being a wife, and I wanted my marriage, but it just worked against me, and I could not save it by myself.

So here I am today, all alone. I have confessed my sins to God, and now it has been over two years I have not been with a man; I am celibate and making that decision sets me apart from foolishness. I can see it! I can see when a man wants me for sex and laughing; but seriously, I probably would have had one by now if that's what I wanted. I often felt like and asked myself if I could get a man right now going through what I am going through. At first, I was thinking no, but now I see differently. I absolutely can. I am still fearfully and wonderfully made by Christ Jesus, and when it is God's time, He will send me who he wants me to have. I know I deserve a good man that will love me unconditionally and to love God just as I do. I will continue to wait.

Being single and celibate is not so bad, but I want somebody to love, I cannot lie. But I will continue to wait on God.

Okay, about that time again; I'm going to Philadelphia this week. I am having my six weeks follow up from radiation. I was diagnosed again for the fourth time now. I had three tumors on my brain and a couple on my lungs. I had an MRI and CT scan, and I was getting my results the following day. Well, I got them, and they were good. My radiation oncologist said the test showed all the spots had shrunk on my brain. I was so happy and so grateful. I said, "Thank you, Jesus!

Walking On Water
Pamela R. Bradley

THE PAIN AND THE HURT

I was going through so much hurt and pain. Toxic relationships will fester in your spirit if you are not aware of it. Try to heal from it and let it go. There is no rhyme or reason as to why we catch different diseases, but not thinking about how it could play a part in your stress level, and it could be somewhat of a cause. Let go of anything that may cause you any stress. It is not worth holding on to any longer. When I spoke to a very spiritual friend, she said let go of everything that has caused you pain. She asked me questions about family and friends. She told me to talk to them and make everything right with everyone quickly. I needed nothing holding me down in my spirit. As I shared my feelings with some people, I opened up and felt the weight coming off. Often, we are not aware of some things until someone brings it to our attention. My attitude was, I didn't want to die with anything unsaid. I tried to fix everything and wanted to make peace in my spirit. As I healed, God restored my body to good health. I went back to church, and I started getting out more. I felt like my confidence was slowly coming back. Did I have insecurities, I sure did. I wasn't comfortable with doing things by myself the thought of it was very scary.

We take so many things for granted. I lost range of motion in my neck so I couldn't turn it like normal. I said to God, why would you take that from me. I couldn't turn my neck. I couldn't open up my mouth wide enough to bite a sandwich. I just knew that would eventually change. Well, it did, but it was not like normal, and after days and months of crying about it. One day the weight was lifted, I no longer worried about it anymore. It became easy to handle or accept. That's God. I was finally living with my new normal.

I often wonder why, I'm still questioning God, why me, but now I say to myself, why not me. God chose me for such a time as this, whatever your will is God let your will be done in my life.

I wondered what I should be eating. I received advice from so many people I was so overwhelmed. People would ask me all the time what am I doing, and some people would challenge me as if I'm responsible for my condition. Little did they know I was crying inside because I was still saying why me God. After the 4th time, I was shocked. I felt like God you want me to do this

Walking On Water
Pamela R. Bradley

again? I know you know how much we can bear, but I promise I wanted to say okay God, this is enough, I don't want to do this anymore, please heal my body God and make me whole, please God I want this behind me.

In Isaiah 53:5, it says God was bruised, and he was wounded, and by his stripes, we are healed. When I think of what God went through I said okay God you went through way more than what I'm going through, God said why not you, I'm walking in my healing no matter what, God healed me once and I'm standing on it, yes his blood still works it still heals. So I Praise him for the blood, his blood still works.

After being rediagnosed with Cancer, they found three tumors on my brain and two tumors on my lungs. I had one treatment of radiation, I prayed and prayed, but honestly, I didn't want radiation anymore, the thought of them putting that mask over my face scared me. I had to act like I was strong knowing I was scared. My prayer was, please God, let the tumors disappear. Please, I don't want radiation again, but it happened anyway. I began to negotiate with God, I said ok God, since you allowed me to have radiation, please don't take my hair out again. Some people will comment like it's just hair it will grow back, but that was beside the point, any woman will get her hair cut, but when it falls out that's another whole situation. But God blessed me, my hair came out a little bit, but I could cover it up. I trust God, no matter how he blesses me. If he did nothing else for me, he has shown me what he can do. God is faithful to his word. He said he would restore my body back to good health. He said I shall live and not die, and I'm living my best life because of God, so when you see me in the streets, be happy because you're looking at a miracle. I am that miracle, to God be the Glory for all he has done for me.

This year, April 2019, I had my first speaking engagement. I was asked to speak in a Woman's Program. I didn't know that I would be diagnosed with Cancer for the fourth time. The program was about the 12 keys to God's resources. I chose determination so befitting for what I'm going through now. The definition of determination is the firmness of purpose. When I decided on the word determination, I did not know that word is what I was living right now. I was so determined to live a healthy life again. I'm so determined to get up every day and feel like nothing has ever happened. To wake up and not feel like nothing is wrong with my neck. To jump up like normal and get ready quickly and hit the street to do whatever I need to do. I want to live my best life with my kids and my granddaughter, but more important, I'm trusting

Walking On Water
Pamela R. Bradley

God, knowing he will never leave me nor forsake me. And I know I'm covered by his blood.

Walking On Water
Pamela R. Bradley

LIVING WITH CANCER

I was living with Cancer. I never would've imagined I would have to live with cancer. When the doctors told me I would have to stay on the Chemo drug I thought by now I would be off of it. Every three weeks for the past three years, I have had IV injections. How have my veins held up? After two years passed, I ran into a problem in and out of the hospital it was horrible. The nurses in the hospital had a problem finding a good vein, and they stuck me several times, it got to where I could not take it anymore.

I told the nurse to stop, please, do not stick me anymore. I asked her to get another nurse. They didn't like it when I spoke up, and they just expected me to sit there and take it. My last time in the hospital, they gave me a second line temporary, and my next step was a Port. The port lasted for a second. I stayed positive. I wanted it to work because I didn't want to go back to the IV again. A few weeks of the surgery, it wasn't healing the way it should, and after two weeks, it got Infected, only God who has kept me. The infection could have been my life. I drove myself to the hospital just in time. I was brave and went by myself because I had no idea it was so severe. I knew I was going back home, but instead, they admitted me into the hospital. They gave me antibiotics first and then decided it had to come out. After a few days passed, they scheduled me for surgery with local anesthesia, and it was over quickly. I was scared, but I knew I had to trust in God. All I could say was Pam, remember that mustard seed faith. I knew I had that, so I stood on it.

After they took my Port out I had made up in my mind, "I said change your mindset, Pam, so what you still have to take Chemo. Some people say it's the worst thing ever, it's hard on your body, and I knew all of that. I found myself explaining to people why I still have to take Chemo to the point where I said stop it. You owe no one an explanation. I'm still living with Cancer and have to continue to take Chemo. My life has been great. I'm feeling almost Like myself. I started asking God, what is it that you would have for me to do. So I began to think about what I could do? I started asking around seeing if anyone needed my help or needed any volunteers because I knew I wasn't looking for a job just something for me to do. I felt like helping someone and making a difference with my new normal as they call it. I searched around for a while, but nothing came up. I prayed and asked God, and then he placed me in places

Walking On Water
Pamela R. Bradley

I've never been. One door after another was opening, and at first, I did not realize what was happening. I got phone calls for me to share my testimony. It seemed like every time I would speak; it was always someone there to ask me to speak somewhere else. I knew God was using me to witness to draw his people to him, I felt like I had to prepare to talk, I would always rewrite my notes every time, and one time God said Pam, don't keep writing things down speak from your heart it's already in you, just show up, and I will do the rest. I have had amazing moments. All is to God be the glory for all he has done. God said he would never leave me nor forsake me. Every day when I awoke, I knew I was blessed because God had saved me from what could have happened, and I am grateful.

Walking On Water
Pamela R. Bradley

Made in the USA
Lexington, KY
30 October 2019

56121468R00033